Tortoise

45 messages inspired by tortoises

Stacey Clarke

ISBN-13: 978-1720608974
ISBN-10: 1720608970

Introduction

This book is full of words of wisdom gathered from my tortoises Splitz, Spot and Munch. It is designed so that the wisdom is applicable to everyday things you might feel or need a little help with.

The images are all drawn by myself in a fun design that is intended to help you remember the key message behind the wisdom.

I would personally use this book almost like you would a set of oracle cards, using your intuition to open it to the page you feel is right for today. Alternatively you can browse through it, finding out which messages may help you with whatever is confusing you at this point in time.

You may also learn a little bit about tortoises, and will undoubtedly look at tortoises in a different way from now on.

Have fun, let the tortoises guide you and please do visit my website and Facebook page for more wisdom, insight and more from the animals in my life.

Stacey

Namaste xxx

Take it steady and appreciate the little things

Tortoises generally have a leisurely pace to life and love to bask in the warmth of the sun. They are also very curious and love to investigate everything. When awake very little escapes their notice as they are present in the moment. Splitz often tells me that I need to take more time to simply 'be' and that even on a bad day there are always little things that can make you smile. For him the everyday simple pleasures of a warm basking spot, fresh food and somewhere dark to dig down for the night are things to appreciate. So think tortoise and take the time to notice the little things that brighten your days even when you feel down in the dumps.

Remember, you are bulletproof

OK so tortoises aren't technically bullet proof, but their hard exterior shell can withstand a lot. I have actually known a tortoise that had dents in his shell that looked very much like he had been hit by gun pellets of some kind in his younger days. He was very much alive and well and going about his days as a normal elderly tortoise would. The message here from all tortoises is to remember you can take a lot more than you first think possible, and if you are going through tough times put a protective energetic shell around yourself and it will help deflect negativity and get you through to the other side.

Meet your obstacles head on

Tortoises approach most things head first by the nature of their body shape. This includes physical barriers, for which the tortoise approach is often to bash into using the front of their shell (head carefully tucked in) to see if they can break through. This is not saying you have to go careering head first into things, but rather in the words of Splitz "no matter how big or small, extraordinary or ordinary the obstacle (physical or mental) blocking your path meet it with determination and be determined to move it, just like the tortoise who head-buts a physical barrier to see if he can get through".

Never stop exploring

Tortoises love to explore. In the wild they would roam for miles looking for food, water, a mate or a good place to sleep safe and sound. In captivity they love to find out what is on the other side of their run, a door, or anything else they realise has more beyond. They don't let much stop them either and are adapt at climbing, burrowing and finding a way through things. Splitz knows it can be difficult to maintain that childhood love of exploring to find out what is on the other side of the fence when you are busy with adult human concerns. However, he encourages us all to never stop exploring, to not lose that childhood curiosity, and to give in to it and see where it takes us. You never know what you might find if you do.

Never give up on your dreams

Splitz, Spot and Munch may appreciate the simple life, but they also have desires and dreams of their own. These can be small, such as the desire for tasty flowers to eat, but can also be larger. Splitz would love a little harem of female tortoises to call his own and although not possible currently (they would need the whole garden to allow them to have space from each other and it's presently not secure enough) he hasn't given up and asks me often how I can help make this dream come true. Tortoises are very determined and Splitz will never give up this dream. He encourages no-one to give up theirs either, as despite obstacles currently there he knows with enough determination that he will get his dream fulfilled.

Never Give Up On Your Dreams!

Believe everyone loves you and they will

Tortoises have an air of confidence I have rarely seen in any other species so consistently. They know who they are and don't care who knows it! They are captivating, sweet and innocent, and bullishly brash at times. They endear many people to them with their glossy eyes, sweet faces and waddle-like walk. Splitz knows I lack confidence sometimes and worry what others think of me. He let me into the secret once of why so many people love tortoises; tortoises believe they are awesome and that they should be loved. The advice here is to believe you are what you want others to see and they will see it.

Confidence comes with practice

Tortoises are generally confident, but like all creatures they gain confidence as they grow and learn. When little they quickly retreat into their shell at the unknown. They are still learning how to maneuver with a solid shell and slopes in particular are difficult, but they don't give up. They keep practicing and eventually learn how to walk up and down slopes without taking a tumble. Before you know it they are running up and down with confidence. So there you have it, the message of the tortoise is to keep trying and practicing, and whatever you feel is impossible and awkward now will get easier and your confidence will grow.

Find your safe place

Tortoises have many safe places. They carry one with them at all times in the form of their shell. They can retreat into this if they feel threatened and have no burrow or other safe place to hide in. A safe place doesn't have to be purely physical though, it can be anywhere you feel comfortable, secure and able to just be you. Spot says finding this place is important for us all and his safe place also happens to be where he can sleep undisturbed.

Sleep is good, spend time rejuvenating

Some species of tortoise sleep for many months to enable them to survive in a climate where the temperature drops to freezing and food is in short supply over winter. This hibernation period also helps to reset their body, helping them to maintain a healthy growth rate. Splitz always says we humans spend too much time rushing around. We should spend more time resting and rejuvenating, just like a tortoise.

If you see something you like, go for it

Tortoises are determined and if they want something they will do everything they can to get it. They don't let anyone tell them they can't have something, especially when it is food related! Their message for us all is simply to go for what you what. When you see something you like or somewhere you want to be don't let anything or anyone stop you from reaching it.

If you see something you like, go for it!

Do what feels natural to you

Splitz can't understand why we humans have toilets, when he needs the loo he just does what comes natural and go's where he is. I'm not suggesting you go the loo where you want, but if something feels artificial or simply plain wrong to you it is probably not for you. Be honest with yourself, do what feels right for you; and what comes naturally is usually a good indication of the things that really fill you with passion, comfort or happiness.

It doesn't matter what others think, as long as you're enjoying it

Remember when you were little and didn't care whether people stared or tut tutted when you splashed in puddles or ran through crisp autumn leaves? Well tortoises don't care what others think no matter how old they get. They go about life enjoying what they are doing, living in the moment. If you enjoy something and it doesn't hurt anyone keep doing it, don't let others negativity make you feel like it is wrong to have fun.

Love the sun, re-energise

Sunshine is amazing at lifting the spirit and for tortoises it is essential to their growth and life. The UV B contained within sunshine helps them to metabolise essential nutrients, especially calcium. This is one reason why tortoises spend so long basking in the sun, but they also enjoy it. Sunshine helps all animals feel energised and happy. So take a leaf from the tortoises' book and spend time simply basking in the suns life giving energy and see how good you can feel.

Flowers are good for you

Splitz loves to eat flowers, especially yellow ones. His face lights up when he smells a flower in his dinner and he chops down with glee. Many flowers (and other parts of plants) are also good for humans. Just think of the benefits of chamomile and peppermint for instance for good gut health and relaxation. Flowers are also good for your mental health; they are beautiful in colour and smell, and are the essence of summer days in country gardens. If you are feeling low go and spend some time with flowers, either those growing from the earth or some cut flowers in a vase. Just concentrate on the flower and let it relax your mind. You might even find you get inspiration from the beauty of the bloom.

Listen to your gut

Many animals know what food and minerals will help them stay healthy and tortoises are no exception. They will seek out plants growing in calcium rich soil as they know that calcium is essential for their proper growth and development. They will also avoid food that has been sprayed with anything by humans, even if this was some time ago. They know what they need by gut instinct. We humans should also listen to our gut, both when it comes to what food we should eat and when we feel something is not quite right. Trust your gut instinct.

Live slow, live long

Tortoises are known for their long life spans. They are also (somewhat mistakenly) known for being rather slow in movement. I can attest to the fact that they aren't always slow, but it is true that they live life at a rather peaceful pace and if they don't want to move fast there is nothing you can do to make them. It is also true that hummingbirds, mice and other creatures that live faster paced lives often live shorter lives. So take note of the tortoise and slowdown from time to time, it may just help you live longer.

Stop for nothing until you get where you want to be

We all have goals and dreams, but there are many distractions along the way. This is true for tortoises too. They might see a lovely flower that would be really tasty, but on the way there is clover, dandelions and a frog to sniff at. Now they could stop at each one and by the time they get to the flower it has been eaten by another. Or they could go straight for the flower and get their dream food, and then go back and try the other options. This is a lesson for life; if there is somewhere you want to be don't get distracted by other desirable things along the way that could mean you miss out on your greatest desire. Remember you can always go and try the other things another time if you still want to once you are happily where you want to be.

Test the waters gently before jumping in

Although often curious and confident tortoises are cautious around new experiences until they have them figured out. Spot urges caution when you are not sure, and to gently check things out until you feel sure it is safe. It doesn't mean all new experiences are bad, most will be good, but you can ensure they are all good by employing a little caution.

Test The water Gently 'Brrrr'
Before Jumping In

Break down barriers

When they come across a physical barrier the tortoise approach is often to bash into it to see if they can break through. You would be surprised by how much power there is in a tortoise body. With the force of a run up and ramming motion behind them they can crack seemingly impossible barriers. Sulcata tortoises (one of the largest species) can crack open a wooden fence with ease. Of course not all barriers are physical and tortoises are adept at solving mental challenges too, including those of communication. Splitz has ways to tell me when something is good or not to his liking – mainly through sometimes subtle body language, or if I don't listen a painful nip. You too can break down barriers, even when they seem as complicated as communication between a human and a tortoise!

Take life in small bites until you're ready for big ones

Baby tortoises can only eat small bits of food at any one time, but this doesn't stop them trying to bite chunks out of leaves that are bigger than they are. However, they soon learn how to manage their food and to break off only what they can chew. As they grow they can eat a lot more in one go, but can still sometimes put too much into their mouth at once. The moral here: take things steady, and take small bites of life until you feel confident to take larger ones without struggling. Before you know it you'll be taking life in large bites without any problems.

Keep a steady pace

Tortoises like to take things steady and conserve their energy. They are good at endurance – just think of the fable 'the tortoise and the hare'. If you feel things are getting out of control and you are exhausted try slowing down until you reach a pace that is more comfortable for you. You will find that if you keep going steady you will get the same, if not more, done without compromising your health and wellbeing.

Keep A steady Pace

Keep yourself grounded

Tortoises, like many reptiles, are very grounded and down to earth. They are always 'in the moment' and love nothing more than to spend time snoozing in a sunny spot leisurely watching the world go by. Being relaxed is a big part of a tortoise's life, and my three little ones Splitz, Spot and Munch always tell me to slow down and get more grounded. There is nothing better than spending time outdoors basking the sun surrounded by flowers, trees and those you love. This applies equally to humans or tortoises!

Remember, you know best for you

Whether it comes to where they sleep, what they eat and who they make connections with, tortoises instinctively know what is best for them and their health. This is also true for humans; we know deep down what is right for us, both on a day to day basis and for our life path. If you have been drawn here today it is likely you are being led in a direction that is not necessarily where you want to go. Trust your instincts and if it doesn't feel right remember: just like the tortoise, you know what is best for you as an individual in this life.

No, I'm a chef

You shoud be a teacher.

Remember, you know best for you

Have a good stretch

When you wake up the first you want to do is to stretch. Tortoises
are no different. Stretching is good for the body as it allows
muscles to reset after being in one position for too long.
Stretching is also good for the mind, it helps us relax and releases
feel good hormones. Yoga involves lots of stretching and tortoises
spend a good proportion of their morning routine stretching into
different positions under the sun. The message here is to make
stretching part of your morning routine and see how more awake
and ready to face the day you feel after a week or so. Stretch and
smile.

No-one is stronger than you

Tortoises are immensely strong for their size. I will always remember one male sulcata tortoise who was so big and strong he could walk under a full wheelbarrow and it would be stuck on his broad shell as he carried on walking. He didn't even notice. In general tortoises don't let anything make them feel small, they are strong physically and mentally and they know it. So if you are feeling small think of the male sulcata tortoise who could carry wheelbarrows on his back, and remember no-one is stronger than you.

Never stop trying

Sometimes it can seem as though you will never get anywhere and that you are banging your head against a brick wall. Remember though, tortoises are determined and even brick walls don't stop them. They try and try until they get where they want to be, and so should you. Maybe the way you are going about things isn't working, maybe you need to change tactics, or maybe you just need more practice. Whatever the reason, don't give up, you will get there.

Be in it for the long haul

Life can be trying and there will be days when you just want to go back to bed. Tortoises have days like that to, but they know that life is a journey and that you need to look for the good in the world and be thankful for even the little things in life, like clean water and fresh food. Life should be long and lived to the full. To do this you need the determination to be in it for the long haul, as well as for the good bits that often seem to fly by.

Be in it for the
long haul

Traverse the elements

Splitz loves the sun, but he doesn't mind the rain either as long as it is warm enough. Tortoises live in many environments and turtles live both in water and on land; they literally traverse the elements throughout their lives. We humans might not have to learn to live with wet and dry conditions (we have houses and waterproof clothes for instance), but we do have to learn to traverse society and the expectations of others. This can be confusing and at times can feel like moving from land (where we are comfortable) to water (less comfortable). If this resonates with you remember the turtles, and Splitz who loves the sun but doesn't mind the rain.

Traverse the Elements

Weeds are good for the planet

Weeds are plants humans see as growing where they are not wanted such as the dandelion in the flowerbed. To many other animals weeds are food, provide nourishment, have medicinal properties and have kept generations of tortoises alive and well. Weeds are also often native to where they grow which is why they do so well. As with all plants weeds provide animals with oxygen, take up carbon dioxide, and they have any properties of use to everyone whether that is medical, fiber, food and drink or simply looking pretty. Be honest, dandelion flowers are bright yellow, they bring a smile to your face, they herald spring. So yes, weeds are good for the planet, and for tortoises! Don't be so quick to judge the humble weed in the future.

Nurture yourself

Spend some time on yourself every day. Tortoises are good at giving themselves time to just be, looking out for themselves and what is best for them. This is something we should all try to do each day, spend some time on ourselves, nurturing our soul and what is important to us. By nurturing yourself you will benefit your mind, body and soul.

Nurture Yourself

Share with your family

Tortoises don't always like to share and can be very solitary
creatures. But when there is enough food to go around they will
happily munch along side by side. They also appreciate company
at times, to share their troubles, to feel safe and secure as they
snooze in the sun, and to learn from. So share with your family,
whether that is blood family or the family you make for yourself.
Share the good and the bad. After all, family is there to support
you and in return you support your family.

Have fun always

Spot and Munch believe that you should enjoy all that you do. You should look for the fun elements of even day to day tasks, and make sure all you do is fun for you and makes you smile. In their eyes there is no point being miserable and you should always try to have fun. Now I know not every day can be a party, but if you take their advice and try to see even the smallest bit of fun in everyday tasks then you will slowly start to look forward to doing them a little more, or at least find them less of a chore.

Flowers are food for the soul

For tortoises flowers can literally be food, although not all flowers are edible. People can eat some flowers too and many of us enjoy flower based products like honey. But flowers are also pretty, colourful and herald spring and summer and sunny warm weather. They raise our spirits and clam our minds, taking us back to lazy summer days of childhood. They are nourishing in so many ways. They are food for body, mind and soul.

Keep going forwards

Tortoises prefer to travel head first. They also prefer to not have to change direction because of obstacles in their path. Splitz, Spot and Munch have all told me to 'keep going forwards' even when it seems tough and all I want to do is lie down and hide from the world. Feel the determination of the tortoise in your veins when you need a hand to get through the day, and push on forwards. Tortoises always get where they want to go eventually, and so will you.

Keep hold of what you want

This can apply to food (a juicy flower is worth holding on to even when your buddy wants a bite), or to anything really. If you have found something or someone you want keep hold of don't let other people's views and opinions make you give up what you have because they think they should have it more, or that it is not good for you. You know what you want, what makes your heart sore and your face split into a grin. Once you have found it, don't let it go. But remember you can share with fellow tortoises (or people).

Encourage others to follow your path

Splitz is a leader and an inspiration. He also encourages me to follow my path where it is for the highest good of all. He encourages me to learn new things, to help as many others as I can, and to encourage others along a healing route. So if you are following the healing route but are unsure what others will think, take inspiration from Splitz and don't be afraid to encourage others to follow it too.

You can find a way out of anything

Tortoises are brilliant escape artists. I have known tortoises who can climb ladders, use tree trunks to get over fences, and dig under wire even when sunk into the ground. Splitz is also good at getting out of boxes, including his hibernation box, even when it's in the fridge and he's supposed to be asleep! The lesson here, don't let things limit you. Tortoises are not exactly built for climbing, and yet they do, regularly. They are also inquisitive and very clever. Use your intuition, your physical and mental abilities to help you find a way out, even when you feel the situation is impossible. Nothing is impossible if a tortoise can climb a ladder!

Nothing is impossible

There are times when we all feel things are impossible and we will never get where we want to be. When life feels like this remember that tortoises end up on their backs sometimes with their feet in the air. This is not a good place to be for a tortoise; your lungs are being squished, you are vulnerable to attack, to cooking in the heat, and you can't move easily. They do not give up however and even baby tortoises can turn themselves back over. It may take some time and sometimes a helping hand/foot/well placed rock to roll against, but they make it back on their feet. So remember, if a tortoise can turn itself over from its back, then nothing is as impossible as it first appears.

Nothing is impossible

I make my own destiny

Each of us is responsible for our own life and what we make of it. We can ask for help along the way, but in the end we need to decide what we want out of life and what we can offer the world in this lifetime. Tortoises are very independent and know what they are after, where they are going and their end goal. Take head from the tortoises and make your own destiny.

I may not be the fastest, but that's no reflection on my intelligence

Tortoises are not known to be fast (they can be, just not often) and in the human world being slow is often associated with having poor intelligence. That is of course not the case. We are all individuals and just because you may feel like you are not moving forward in life as fast as someone else it doesn't mean you are doing something wrong, or don't deserve the best life has to offer. Remember, you have all you need inside you. Taking your time to figure things out does not make you slow, it means you are giving yourself time to get to know yourself and consider all options available to you. This is intelligence at work.

Be brave

Bravery comes in many forms. It all depends on where you are starting from. You don't have to be a superhero to be brave. You were brave the first day you went to school, when you stood up for a friend, when you moved out of your family home, when you asked that sweet someone on a date. Yes, the everyday things we do through life can be brave. Splitz knows this, he has had three homes in his life so far and each time he sticks his neck out from his shell, says hello and tries to make friends with everyone. Sticking your neck out in a tortoises' case is brave as it exposes soft skin, key blood vessels and breathing tubes. So be brave in your decisions. Even the little ones count and you never know where they might lead.

Break out of your egg; it's only a barrier if you let it be one

The first big task in a tortoise's life is to get out of their egg. This is a physical barrier they have to break, but I was given this wisdom in the context of psychological barriers. We all build up walls around us without even being aware of it. We retreat to safe places within ourselves and fall back on safe patterns of behaviour when things get uncomfortable. We in effect retreat back into our own egg. The problem with falling back on what has worked before may mean you can't get to where you want to be. To get there you need to be brave and push out of your comfort zone. You need to break down self-built barriers and break out of your egg.

Break out of
your egg...

It's only a barrier
if you let it be
one!

Know who you are

Tortoises are very sure of themselves. Splitz, Spot and Munch know that they are individual tortoises, that they live on land, eat vegetation and that they each have their own special place in my heart. They know they are not turtles either! They say it is important to know who you are too, who you really are inside, what makes you tick. Get to know your true self.

Follow the sunshine

Sunshine is a tortoise's best friend. It provides their life giving heat and UV rays that help them metabolise food and grow. Splitz follows the sunlight around his enclosure during the day, making sure he sleeps where the last rays will keep him warm for longest, or where he can move easily to catch the first rays of sun the following morning. Sunshine is also brilliant for moods, which is why most of us feel sad in winter; we don't have as much access to the life giving rays of sunshine as we do in summer. So when you can follow the sunshine, or bring little reminders of it into your home such as pretty crystals and flowers, paint brightly coloured walls or hang tapestries of sunny scenes.

Follow the Sunshine

I appreciate everything, even the smelly stuff

Splitz is quite fond of things I don't like the smell of, like his own pungent scent. However, I know that if he is making poop then he is eating, and if it smells as normal then he has a healthy gut. Poop is a good way to tell the health of your gut and so I have learnt that although it smells bad to appreciate the information it gives me about my animals' health. What I am trying to say here is that even something that seems nasty on the surface can have a use and can even be something that can make you smile (like when I know all my animals are doing healthy poop). So try to appreciate the things you don't much like, even if only as a learning experience.

I appreciate everything...

Pacco

Even the smelly Stuff!

Acknowledgements

Thank you to Spliz, Spot and Munch for their help with inspiring me to write this book. Thank you also to the many other tortoises I have known who have inspired certain tales here.

Finally, thank you to my husband for looking after the tortoises and many other animals we share our home with, especially when I am away with the day job.

16795458R10028

Printed in Great Britain
by Amazon